Build a Birdhouse

BY MIRELLA S. MILLER · ILLUSTRATED BY ROGER STEWART

Published by The Child's World®
1980 Lookout Drive · Mankato, MN 56003-1705
800-599-READ · www.childsworld.com

Acknowledgments
The Child's World®: Mary Swensen, Publishing Director
Red Line Editorial: Editorial direction and production
The Design Lab: Design

Photographs ©: Shutterstock Images, 5, 7; Alexandrra Giese/
Shutterstock Images, 6; Marty Pitcairn/Shutterstock Images, 8;
iStockphoto, 9

Design Elements: JosephTodaro/Texturevault; Shutterstock Images

ISBN 9781503807839

LCCN 2015919409

Printed in the United States of America
Mankato, MN
June, 2016
PA02301

ABOUT THE AUTHOR

Mirella S. Miller is an author and editor of several children's books. She lives in Minnesota with her husband and their dog.

ABOUT THE ILLUSTRATOR

Roger Stewart has been an artist and illustrator for more than 30 years. His first job involved drawing aircraft parts. Since then, he has worked in advertising, design, film, and publishing. Roger has lived in London, England, and Sydney, Australia, but he now lives on the southern coast of England.

Contents

CHAPTER ONE

Birds and People

Taking care of the **environment** can mean many different things. You might recycle to help cut back on waste. Or your family might have a garden in your yard. But taking care of the environment can also mean protecting Earth's animals. Birds are common animals seen in yards and parks. There are hundreds of types of birds in North America alone.

Many types of birds need shelter to live in, especially during winter. Some birds build houses in nature. They might use holes in trees to

CHEMICALS AND BIRDS

Chemicals are often used in yards. They help get rid of bugs and weeds but can hurt birds. There are natural ways to help your yard that won't hurt birds. For example, you can release ladybugs in your yard. They eat pests such as aphids. You can also grow your grass longer. Doing this keeps weeds such as crabgrass from growing. Talk to your parents about how to use fewer chemicals in your yard.

make nests. But many bird **habitats** are being destroyed. Humans cut down trees to make things. When many trees are cut down, there might not be enough natural bird homes. Birds without homes might die or be forced to move away from an area. Humans can help birds by making new shelters and putting them outside. Birds can safely return to these homes. Birdhouses can help bird populations grow.

In nature, nesting birds often live in holes in trees.

CHAPTER TWO

The Benefits of a Birdhouse

A birdhouse is a good home for birds. Female birds can lay their eggs in birdhouses. Birdhouses keep the birds and their eggs safe from **predators**. The bird population may grow if bigger animals cannot hunt the eggs. Snakes and raccoons are some of the animals birds must watch out for.

Some birds fly south to warmer weather in the winter. They use birdhouses to rest along the way. But not all birds fly south. Others stay in cold places. Birdhouses help keep these birds warm. The birds may sleep close together in birdhouses. Doing so helps birds stay warm.

Birdhouses can keep birds safe and warm during winter.

Having birdhouses in yards or parks helps the surrounding environment. Many birds that nest in birdhouses eat insects. These birds control the numbers of worms, flies, and mosquitoes. This helps keep bugs from bothering humans and plants. Birds also help keep unwanted weeds from growing. They eat weed

Birds help clear people's yards of unwanted pests.

seeds. Birds also help flowers. Birds spread pollen between flowers. This helps the plants make seeds.

People enjoy having birds around for other reasons, too. Many people like to learn about birds. They identify different types of birds and watch their movements. Some people like to have birds around because they think the birds are beautiful.

CHAPTER THREE

Planning the Perfect Home

It is important to pick a good spot to hang a birdhouse. You can hang it from a tree branch. Or you can attach it to a pole or a tree trunk. A birdhouse should be at least 20 feet (6 m) from any bird feeders or birdbaths. These places are often noisy. Birds want their nests to be quiet.

It is also important to do research before building a birdhouse. The opening of the birdhouse needs to be the right size. Some birds look

Birdhouses should be placed away from busy bird feeders.

HELPING BIRDS

Ask your parents to help you plant native plants in your yard. These are plants that grow naturally in your area. Native plants attract birds. You might also suggest keeping leaf or grass piles outside. Birds use these materials for nests.

for houses with small openings. Other birds need larger openings. Birds need to be able to enter the birdhouse. But the opening must not be too big. If it is, predators might get inside. Once a bird finds the right birdhouse, it will build a nest. Birds use feathers, twigs, grass, and moss to make their nests.

Squirrels may eat bird eggs.

CHAPTER FOUR

Building a Birdhouse

Helping birds is easy. You can build a birdhouse with materials from around the house. Turning old materials into something new is called repurposing. You will help birds with your new creation. You will also be helping the environment by using repurposed materials. The carton you will use is being reused. You can use a rag or a piece of old fabric for the cloth. You can also use repurposed items to decorate your birdhouse.

Gather your materials. Then find a flat surface to work on. Cover the area with newspaper to help keep it clean. As you work, make sure you ask an adult for help when you need it. Let's get started!

REPURPOSING

Using old materials makes it so you do not need to buy new things. It also means you do not need to throw away as much. When we throw things away, it takes work to make them into usable objects again. And many things cannot be remade. These objects are put into **landfills**. The sites are bad for the environment.

MATERIALS

- ☐ Half-gallon milk carton
- ☐ Stapler
- ☐ Hole punch
- ☐ Scissors
- ☐ Ruler
- ☐ Roll of masking tape
- ☐ Cloth or rag
- ☐ Brown shoe polish

- ☐ Decorating materials, such as buttons, sticks, stickers, or pipe cleaners
- ☐ Glue
- ☐ 7-inch (18 cm) stick
- ☐ 1 foot (30 cm) of **twine**
- ☐ Handful of twigs, pine needles, bark, or grass

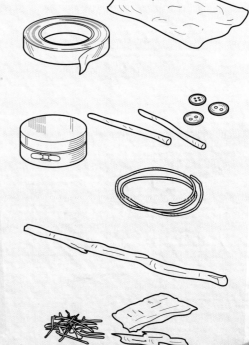

11

INSTRUCTIONS

STEP 1: Empty the carton. Rinse it out with water. Once it is dry, close the top flap. Staple it shut.

STEP 2: Take the hole punch. Make a hole in the center of the top flap.

STEP 3: Turn the carton 90 degrees. The top of the carton should make an upside down Y shape.

STEP 4: Take your scissors. Cut a circular entrance into this side of the carton. Make sure the hole is the right size for the bird you researched. A good size for many birds is 1.5 inches (3.8 cm). The bottom of the opening should be about 4 inches (10 cm) from the bottom of the carton. Use your ruler to check.

STEP 5: Use the hole punch to make a hole .5 inches (1.3 cm) below the opening. On the opposite side of the carton, make another hole. You will need to use the scissors for the second hole. Make sure the holes line up. The holes should be big enough for the stick to fit through.

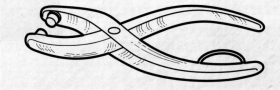

STEP 6: Turn the carton upside down. Use the scissors to make four small holes in the bottom of the carton. These will keep water from collecting in the bottom of the birdhouse. Rain that falls into the carton will drain out of the holes.

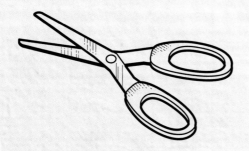

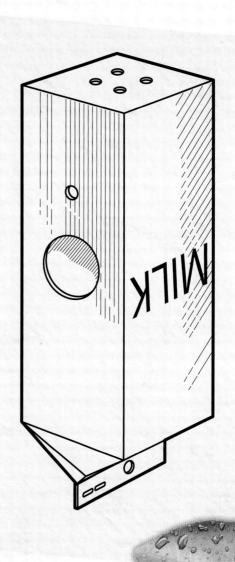

STEP 7: Now it is time to decorate the birdhouse! Cover the carton with strips of masking tape. Place the strips side by side. The strips can overlap. When you get to the big opening, wrap the ends of the tape around the edges. After the carton is covered, use scissors to poke through the smaller holes.

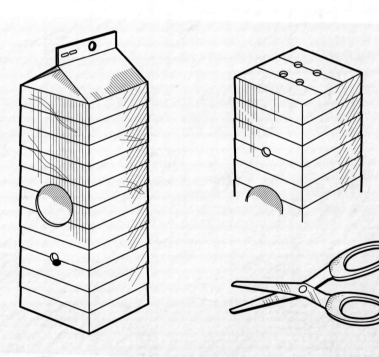

STEP 8: Take the cloth. Use it to rub shoe polish over the tape. Let the carton dry. The tape and shoe polish will help the carton last longer. They will also make the birdhouse look more like a home.

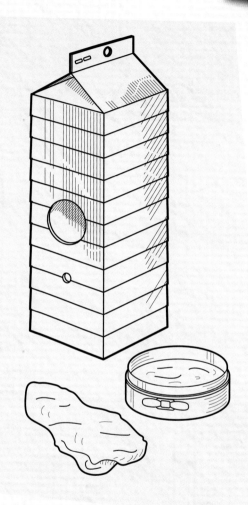

GETTING CREATIVE

If you do not have brown shoe polish, you can use other materials to decorate your birdhouse. Try using strips of duct tape. It comes in many colors and patterns. You can also add shiny decorations. These attract birds.

STEP 9: Use your other materials to decorate more. Add buttons to make flowers on the carton. Or use sticks to make windows. You may need to use glue.

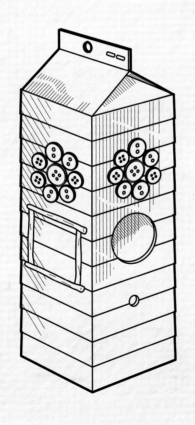

STEP 10: Insert the stick into the hole below the opening of the carton. Feed the stick through to the other hole. The birds will use the stick as a **perch**.

NO YARD? NO PROBLEM!

Some houses or apartments do not have yards. Or you might not have trees in your yard. Have an adult place a plant hook on a deck or outside a window. Then hang your birdhouse from the hook.

STEP 11: Find twigs, pine needles, bark, or grass from the area. Place them in the bottom of the birdhouse. These items can help birds start their nests.

STEP 12: Find a place outside to hang your birdhouse. Pick a spot you can easily see. Take the twine. Cut off a piece. Make sure it will be long enough. Thread the twine through the hole in the top of your birdhouse. With an adult's help, use the twine to hang the birdhouse.

STEP 13: Birds use birdhouses to raise their young. Birds do not like to use the same nest more than once. After birds are finished nesting in your birdhouse, you can build a new birdhouse.

GLOSSARY

chemicals (KEM-uh-kuhls) Chemicals are substances used in or made by chemistry. Human-made chemicals can be unsafe for birds.

environment (en-VYE-ruhn-muhnt) The environment is the natural world. It is important to take care of the environment.

habitats (HAB-uh-tats) Habitats are the places where plants or animals normally grow or live. Some birds live in cold habitats all year.

landfills (LAND-fils) Landfills are places where garbage is collected and buried. Material in landfills breaks down slowly.

perch (PURCH) A perch is a resting place for a bird. The stick on your birdhouse is a perch.

predators (PRED-uh-turs) Predators are animals that kill and eat other animals. Birds have many predators.

twine (TWINE) Twine is string that is made from two or more threads twisted together. Use twine to hang your birdhouse outside.

TO LEARN MORE

In the Library

Danielson, Ethan. *Inside Bird Nests*. New York: PowerKids, 2016.

Friday, Megan. *Green Crafts: Become an Earth-Friendly Craft Star, Step by Easy Step!* Mankato, MN: Black Rabbit, 2011.

Rau, Dana Meachen. *Creating Crafts from Nature*. Ann Arbor, MI: Cherry Lake, 2016.

On the Web

Visit our Web site for links about birdhouses:
childsworld.com/links

*Note to Parents, Teachers, and Librarians:
We routinely verify our Web links to make sure
they are safe and active sites. So encourage
your readers to check them out!*

INDEX